The Girlfriends' Bible on Dating, Mating, and Other Matters of the Flesh

Cathy Hamilton

Andrews McMeel Publishing

Kansas City

06 07 08 09 10 SHD 10 9 8 7 6 5 4 3 2 1

ISBN-13: 978-0-7407-5675-7
ISBN-10: 0-7407-5675-3

Library of Congress Control Number: 2005933691

www.andrewsmcmeel.com

The Girlfriends' Bible trademark is owned by Vicki Iovine and is licensed to Andrews McMeel Publishing, LLC.

ATTENTION: SCHOOLS AND BUSINESSES
Andrews McMeel books are available at quantity discounts with bulk purchase for educational, business, or sales promotional use. For information, please write to: Special Sales Department, Andrews McMeel Publishing, LLC, 4520 Main Street, Kansas City, Missouri 64111.

Contents

In the beginning
there were girlfriends.

The
Book of
Suzanne

For Eve, after receiving Adam's rib (a rib that was two sizes too big for her, thus forcing her into a bigger bra size), was sitting idly in the Garden of Eden, contemplating her navel and suffering from dire hunger (for Adam was not much in the hunting-and-gathering department), when she was approached by the serpent, Suzanne, who admonished Eve, saying, "Girl, it's a sin to shop on an empty stomach. Munch on this apple and let's go check out the new fig leaves at the Genesis store. It's Ladies' Night at Rock of Ages!" So Eve fled the Garden with Suzanne, leaving Adam to fend for himself. And, thus, the girlfriends set out on an eternal quest for the perfect outfit and the ideal man.

Fear not, for I am your girlfriend. And I shall not fear, for you are mine.

Together we shall roam Creation in search of the perfect man, even though we know he may not exist of this earth. For we are nothing if not incurable romantics with exalted expectations. And it is good.

And we shall hold ourselves and our men to the highest standards because we deserve nothing less. For to compromise our ideals in men would be akin to choosing shoes with man-made uppers over real leather, just to save a few pennies, and not only is that a sin against nature, it is ludicrous.

And it shall be ordained that the perfect man will possess an abundance of intelligence, courage, honesty, fidelity and charm as well as a smoking hot body and impressive stock portfolio, according to the highest law.

Yea, though we walk through the valley of speed dating and singles' bars, we shall not feel trepidation. For we know that such places are necessary evils in our efforts to weed the bad fruit from the good. And there is beauty, truth, and joy in the weeding. For weeding begets reaping. And we shall reap what we sow.

And we shall decree that it is not sinful, but righteous, to sample the occasional bad fruit, so as to know the good fruit when they come along. And, sometimes, we will find it necessary to sample a multitude of bad fruit, of all varieties, simply because they are firm and ripe and smell delicious, and we should not fear.

Behold, it is wise to savor a variety of men in all shapes, sizes, colors, and creeds. For variety is the spice of life. And spice contains no calories or carbohydrates.

And you will know, without doubt or reservation, that your new man shall not be deemed worthy without inspection by me. And, like-wise, shall you examine my man by the same strict code. Because two heads are better than one. And two pairs of eyes can often find fault where one pair of eyes cannot.

And if you should find a man who is judged to be fitting, I shall say "Yea!" and rejoice with you. And I shall not feel envy, lust, or greed. For you will have someone to protect, please, and pleasure you. And he will most certainly have a friend.

And we shall know for all time that lovers are fleeting, but girlfriends are forever.

The
Book of
Brittany

And thus it was in the days of Lot, the men of Sodom and Gomorrah ate and drank, bought and sold, cheated and fornicated, and, in general, just behaved badly. And Lot was instructed by an angel to flee these evil places, and to take with him his wife, known to all as "Lot's wife," so he should lead her not into temptation. But Lot's wife resisted. She did not want to leave Sodom and Gomorrah. For

she was curiously drawn to evil
men and apparently weary of not
having a first name. Lot grabbed
his wife and led her down the
path toward redemption. But
Lot's wife, whose given name, in
truth, was Brittany, shrugged off
his grasp and turned back for one
last look at the bad men and, thus,
turned into a bitter cautionary
tale, forever to be taken with a
grain of salt.

And, lo, if I shall witness your man coveting another, because she possesses bigger breasts or blonder hair, and you are not there to witness this for yourself, I shall come to you and report what I've seen. For you are my girlfriend, and he is but a snake in the grass. And friends are more righteous than snakes.

When a man that you covet takes you out on a date, and wines you and dines you, and you succumb to him, body and soul, for you are merely mortal and it has been forty days and forty nights since you succumbed to anyone but Ben & Jerry, and he tells you, in dawn's early light, "I'll call you tomorrow" but he does not, cry out to me and I will come to you with chocolate, Cosmopolitans, and the contents of my medicine cabinet.

And when I see that you are waiting fruitlessly, day and night, for your phone to ring, and you seethe with disappointment when it does not, I will reassure you that the man in question was not worthy of you, for he was obviously too unorganized to keep track of one little phone number, and this does not bode well for keeping his future affairs in order. And who amongst us needs that worry?

And, lo, if it comes to pass that the same man calls you, unexpectedly, two weeks later, very late at night, and he desires to come to your abode immediately because he's "dying to see you," I shall remind you, if I am near, that this man is not dying. He is merely afflicted with longing in the nether regions of his physical body and you shall not feel obligated to ease his pain, unless you share the same affliction in *your* physical body.

For this is what is known, far and wide, as a booty call. And it shall be ordained that booty calls shall not come to pass unless they are beneficial for both booties. For if one booty finds gratification and fulfillment from the call but the other booty does not, then one booty has missed its calling. And it will not be good.

But if it *is* good and you desire a multitude of booty calls with this man but do not desire him for intellectual or emotional fulfillment or, heaven knows, holy matrimony, and you are at peace with this, I will not cast aspersions on you or call you a filthy slut. Because only she who is without sluttiness will be permitted by divine law to cast stones, and thus you will suffer no stone-slinging from me.

For are we not mortal women filled with mortal desires? And do we not deserve the occasional joyous moment of rapture that causes us to tremble and shout to the sky the Lord's name? Damn right, we do!

The Book of Eve

And Eve, after sampling apple martinis at Rock of Ages with the serpent Suzanne, returned to the Garden and picked another fruit from the illicit tree. She took a bite and offered it to Adam, who had not, up to that moment, discovered the tree because he refused to ask for directions. And Adam was so hungry he succumbed to temptation and bit into the apple. Suddenly, the sky above them became black, with bolts of lightning. And thunder clapped all around them. God was very angry with Eve for her weakness and at Adam for not being able to find anything to eat in a garden bursting with produce. So God banished Adam and Eve from Paradise, forcing Adam into the charms of Suzanne and Eve to look for a more fruitful relationship.

And we shall know with certainty
which men are fair game and which
are forbidden fruit.

We shall accept as gospel that it is against the natural laws of womankind to commence a relationship with a girlfriend's boyfriend or husband. And this is true even if she claims to despise him and wishes him dead and we firmly believe that we would be granting her an immense favor by proving, into perpetuity, how wrong he was for her.

And, lo, we shall obey the commandment "Thou shall wait at least
two calendar years before becoming
involved with a girlfriend's ex and
then only with her blessing and on
the condition that she was the one
who ended the relationship and is
currently in another healthy and
satisfying love affair, preferably in
another town."

And thus I tell you this, if after
the appropriate waiting period,
I ask for and receive your blessing to
begin a relationship with your ex, I
shall resist the temptation to compare
notes with regards to our intimate
activities, especially those of a coital
nature. For if he should prove to be
the most heavenly man I've ever
known in the biblical sense and your
opinion of his prowess was only so-
so, I will be forever bewildered about
how our standards could be so
diverse, and you will feel the same.

And we shall abide by the commandment that bans us from dating anyone older than our fathers or younger
than our sons. And we will likewise
agree that it is sinful to sleep with a
best friend's father, or a father's best
friend. And I give you my solemn vow
that I will never lie down with your
brother and you will promise never to
lie down with mine. For such a deed
would be foolish, unseemly, and icky.
And it will be so.

And it shall be decreed that the swiftest way to gain a reputation as a slut, no matter how virtuous you are, is to have an affair with the boss, unless a career move is planned in the immediate future. And I shall hold you to this law, and you will do the same unto me.

Be assured that when I witness you showing interest in a man who is obviously on the rebound from another intimate relationship, I will come to you and share my concerns. For men on the rebound are often of unsound mind, even if their bodies are exceedingly sound.

And if I should witness you becoming attracted to a man who is bound by the covenant of marriage, I will rush to your door and remind you that there is but a snowball's chance in hell that he will leave his wife and children for you. And you will believe.

And we will know this universal truth and spread the gospel throughout all girldom: It is impossible to convert a gay man, no matter how heartbreakingly handsome, funny, or stylish, to our team, even though it might be fun to try.

The
Book
of
Zoe

And Noah came to his wife, Zoe, with the ominous news that torrential rain was in the long-range forecast, an imminent flood so wide and deep that it would obliterate all of Creation. Noah told Zoe he had been instructed by God to build a large vessel called an ark so they could ride out the storm. Oh, and by the way, he invited two of every species of animal on the planet, one male and one female, to ride along. Zoe was disturbed by this. She was prone to seasickness and certain that she would be the one cleaning up after all those animals. But she acceded to Noah's wishes and prepared a multitude of bologna sandwiches for the journey. For forty days and forty nights it rained. And Zoe was trapped on a boat with randy lions and tigers and bears and, oh my, Noah, who was the randiest of all. Finally, the waters parted and Zoe disembarked the ark as fast as she could and said unto Noah, "Don't wait up, I'm going out with the girls."

It shall be ordained that "Girls Nights Out" are the sacrosanct birthright of every woman on this earth, married or single, and neither man nor beast shall put limits on these rituals.

And we, in turn, shall not impose restrictions on ourselves during these sacred rites of female bonding. For we shall eat, drink, cavort, and be merry with abandon and without concern about what others might think. And it will be good.

To you, O girlfriend, I make this pledge: If we are out cavorting and searching for men, I will abide by the commandment "She who sees him first gets dibs." And this shall mean that if you see a man whom you covet, and you verbalize your intent aloud to me that you desire this man and want to have babes in swaddling clothes with him, I will honor your wishes because you have seen him first.

And if you and I are at a club, and our cocktail dresses are fine, and a man asks me to dance, I will always seek your permission before I accept. And you will do the same. And it shall be ordained that we will not allow the other to sit alone longer than one dance.

And, lo, if we are approached by two men, both longing to dance, and you say "no" to your man, I will say "no" to mine. For I fear that, whilst I am dancing, the man you rejected might join you at the table, making you more miserable than if you had agreed to dance with him in the first place. The exception to this law shall be if my man is absolutely gorgeous and I believe he might be the man to father my children. Then, it will be your obligation to play the Good Samaritan and dance with his sorry friend.

And when it comes to pass that we lack male companionship but the dance floor beckons and the music pulsates with an irresistible beat, we will dance with each other with our arms raised high and worry not about what others might think.

Should I find you making an alcohol-induced spectacle of yourself on the dance floor, it will be my moral obligation to step in and deliver you from public humiliation and future exposure on *Girls Gone Wild* videos. And you shall do likewise. And we shall forever be flash-free.

Believe this: I will always obtain your approval before inviting a man to join us at our table. And veto power will ultimately be yours, just as it will be mine when the situation is reversed.

Now if it happens that a man you are interested in turns his attention to me, I solemnly vow not to further entice him by exposing my cleavage or my scintillating knowledge of NFL statistics.

And you will have my earnest pledge that I shall never leave a club or party with a man unless I am sure you have a safe ride home or, at the least, sufficient cab fare. And you shall do the same for me.

The
Book
of Mimi

And it came to pass that Naomi, whose friends called her Mimi, was widowed at a ripe young age when her husband, Eli, fatally succumbed to a plague of locusts whilst edging the lawn on a late summer's eve. After a fortnight of mourning, Mimi's friends and family barged into her hut and swarmed around her with names of eligible bachelors from the village. And the names were

Ezekial, Brutus, Abraham, and Dave. And Mimi was very afraid. But her friends showed no mercy. So Mimi meditated and asked God to give her strength and set out on blind faith with a man of her friends' choosing. Blessed is the woman who endures the dreaded fix-up, for she will inherit the dregs of the earth.

And, lo, when I arrange a blind date for you with an eligible acquaintance or fellow worker, and you pose the question "What does he look like?," I will tell you the truth as accurately as possible and be not evasive with phrases like "He's got a great personality!" For you need and deserve to be prepared. And thus you shall be.

And I will earnestly describe your fine points to this man so that he will know you are infinitely wise, exceedingly kind, and desirable to a multitude of men, and that he is the most fortunate man on this earth to have an opportunity to capture your fancy.

I solemnly vow to accompany you on a first date if you are feeling nervous, especially if it is a rendezvous that I have arranged or one that was initiated in cyberspace.

Behold! I will resist the temptation to match you with a man who I know is wrong for you, even if you are desperately horny, over thirty years of age, and it is New Year's Eve.

And together we will understand that it is futile to fix up a girlfriend who is impossible to please. And thus we shall never try.

And if you should arrange a blind date for me and that date is a disaster of epic proportions, I shall not blame you. And you will not blame me if the situation is reversed. For we will know that the catastrophe was wholly the man's fault. Amen.

Hearken to this! Do not offer a man your phone number or personal e-mail address if you hold no intention of seeing him again. For this would only confuse the man. For he, like all his brethren, is confused enough already.

And we shall abide by the three-strikes law regarding fix-ups. For after three unsuccessful attempts, a girlfriend will be on her own.

And if it should happen that by divine intervention the date goes well, and you desire this man and he desires you, I will rejoice for you with gladness in my heart and sing "Hallelujah" because this, indeed, will be a minor miracle.

The Book of Dee

And there lived a beautiful woman named Delilah, or Dee

for short, who met a strapping and handsome man named Sampson. And Sampson, who bore an uncanny resemblance to Fabio, had long flowing hair, strong arms, and sinewy limbs. And Dee, who was a sucker for anything sinewy, gave herself to him, body and soul. But, alas, she soon discovered that Sampson was untrue. He was what was known in biblical times as a "player," a man who had dalliances with many women in their village. So Dee decided she must cut off all contact with Sampson, along with all of his hair. For hell hath no fury like a woman scorned, especially one holding a pair of sheep shears. For Sampson's hair, Dee received a thousand pieces of silver from the village hair-extension maker. And with this silver she splurged on a cornucopia of scented oils, chocolate, and Chianti.

And we shall know that relationships, no matter how blissful or idyllic, often come to a bitter and painful ending. And this, too, shall pass.

Be assured of this very thing. If your romantic relationship should end badly, cry out and I will come hither and listen to your woes all night and agree with every horrendous thing you say about him, whether or not I find it to be true.

Be assured of this very thing. If your romantic relationship should end badly, cry out and I will come hither and listen to your woes all night and agree with every horrendous thing you say about him, whether or not I find it to be true.

When you have suffered a devastating breakup and you embark on a binge of gluttony, lust, greed, and sloth, I will not forsake but join you. For that is what a friend is for. And sometimes, gluttony, lust, greed, and sloth can be one helluva good time.

And when the love of your life jilts you for another, woman, we shall seek and, yea, we shall find this harlot. We will discover her faults by the dozen, and we will recognize that the only reason he abandoned you was because he feared he was no match for your divine perfection. And thus it will be so.

And I shall make this vow to you
this day that, no matter how much
I am tempted, I will never let the
words "I told you so" escape my lips.

And should you betray your man for another, I will not condemn you or question your intentions or your sanity, no matter how much I favored the man, for I will know you must have had a very good reason, even if I cannot fathom what it could be.

Lo, and when I behold you are thinking of dialing the man you forsook, because you have imbibed too many margaritas and are consumed with sexual longing, I will stop you, even if it means applying bodily force, and remind you why you dropped his sorry ass in the first place.

And we will realize that, no matter how badly we are tempted, it would be unwise to ridicule, condemn, or castigate a man after a breakup. For one never knows if future circumstances will bring you together with this man as a boss, opposing counsel, or God forbid, brother-in-law.

For the lesson to be learned in the
breakup parable will always be:
It is just as easy to fall in love with a
good guy as it is a jerk.

The Book of Maggie

And Mary Magdalene, whose nickname was Maggie, was known throughout the land as a woman of ill repute because she possessed great beauty, a voluptuous body, and a penchant for drugstore perfume. But Maggie did nothing that was unlawful, such as accepting pieces of gold for granting bodily favors. She simply had an unfortunate habit of waking up in the tents of strange men after a night of rocking the casbah. This earned her the reputation as a wicked adulteress whilst the men she slept with were, naturally, worshipped as beastly studs.

It shall be decreed thorughout the
land, according to the god Absolut,
that no man ever looks as good in
the light of day as he did the night
before in the darkness of the tavern.

Moreover, it shall be decreed that
sex with a perfect stranger is never
a good plan, even if he seems,
indeed, to be truly perfect.

And I shall remind you, and you in turn shall repeat back to me, that with precious few exceptions, the swiftest way to lose a man's friendship is to sleep with him.

Yet it will also be ordained that casual, indiscriminate kissing is not as sinful as a one-night stand and shall never require the same amount of repentance except, perhaps, if one engages in sloppy open-mouthed kisses with the husband of the deceased at a funeral reception.

And if you come to me, full of remorse and shame, because you succumbed to an impulsive one-night stand, I will reassure you that everyone on earth makes mistakes and remind you of the time I did something equally dimwitted, even if I have to make something up.

And we shall be of the same mind that birth control is ultimately our own responsibility and that men in the throes of passion will say anything to get a woman to lie down in their bed, even going as far as to fabricate a vasectomy or hunting accident.

And I shall remind you of the universal law declaring that if a man invites you into his dwelling after a date, an appeal for sexual relations is always implied. And, thus, you shall not be naive or taken by surprise.

And likewise you will remind me, lest I forget, that to invite a man into your own abode after an evening of food and wine conveys an invitation for him to have sex with you. And we will act accordingly.

And we shall know the difference, however slight, between flirting and teasing. And we shall revel in our flirtations but vow never to tease.

Wherefore this day, we ordain that
it is never prudent to tell a man
how many others you have slept
with, as there is no answer that is
both true and believable.

And we will resist the temptation, no matter how compelling, to phone a man in the wee hours of the night to see if he is at home. For this behavior is neither proper nor righteous nor lawful and caller ID will be our undoing and our shame.

The Book of Rachel

And it came to pass that self-righteous villagers, who did not approve of

Mary Magdalene's licentious behavior, decreed that she be stoned, in the village square. And this was not to be the good kind of stoned, like after a visit to an opium den; they were actually going to pelt her with large rocks. The townsfolk circled around Maggie, preparing to pelt. Suddenly, the fair maiden Rachel, who was passing by on the way to sip coffee with Monica, Chandler, and Joey, cried out and pointed to an unmarried couple kissing, groping, and carrying on across the square by the temple door. "Public display of affection!" Rachel called out. And the crowd turned and moved on the demonstrative lovers, stones held high, chanting "Get a room! Get a room!" And Maggie escaped into the night, owing her freedom to Rachel and the universal law that PDA trumps nooky behind closed doors every time.

Be assured of this: I will not do anything in public with my man, in a
physical way, that you would not
want to witness. And you shall give
me the same deference.

And i say unto you, at no time will I make out, grope, or share in another public display of affection with a man in front of you when you happen to be alone. And there shall be no exceptions to this rule unless, and only unless, it has been several months since I have been kissed and I am mad with desire, or if I have just been told that I have only two months to live.

And we will steadfastly reject gross public displays of affection with strangers at clubs or parties because that is why God created coat closets. And they are good.

We will forever shun the use of cutesy nicknames, cooing, and other baby talk with men, no matter how much love we claim to feel. For we know that such atrocities should never be spoken aloud by adults in public. And this is the word.

And it shall be ordained by the most high that while one's car is stopped at a traffic light, anything more than a quick peck between lovers will be deemed tacky.

And we will know that it is even
tackier, if not death-defyingly
dangerous, to make out while
attempting to drive a motor vehicle.
For that is why God invented cheap
motel rooms.

The Book of Jewel

And Jezebel was known throughout the land as a whore and a

witch, one who seduced men and convinced them to commit fornication, as if men needed convincing in that area. She donned too much makeup and perfume and wrapped her robes too tight around her body. And, sometimes, to tease the scribes and arouse the Pharisees, she would conveniently forget to fasten her veil, revealing her long flowing hair and deep décolletage. And the elders would preach that flesh lusts against spirit and spirit against the flesh, yet she would not repent. For Jezebel felt neither corrupt nor spiritless. She had simply watched too many reruns of *Sex and the City*. But the villagers would not relent and threatened to lock Jezebel in a convent and take away her Manolos. And thus she hightailed it to Gomorrah and changed her name to Jewel.

Whither thou goest, I will go.
Whither thou sleepest, I will never
tell.

For if you are troubled by matters of the flesh, share your sexual escapades with me, sparing no details, and I will not, under any circumstances, share them with others, no matter how juicy or what kind of new techniques I might have learned.

And we shall abide by the law that
states if a girlfriend doesn't kiss and tell,
she has no right to ask.

Wherefore we agree that full
disclosure of one's sexual history
is required of both partners before an
intimate encounter, and if a man is
not willing to reveal the exploits of
his past, we must bid farewell to that
man, regardless of whether he is
wealthy or splendidly endowed.

And should you decide to lie down with a man for a physical coupling, and he does not perform like manna from heaven, I will leadeth you to the nearest tavern and we will drown your sorrows with jugs of wine.

So be it: A girlfriend will be allowed to confer in confidence about her sexual adventures and practices. For this will give her fellow girlfriends the opportunity to learn, advise, and giggle in titillation.

And no girl shall be admonished or demeaned for any controversial sexual behaviors, such as sleeping with a man on a first date, as these are personal matters and, sometimes, hormonal forces are insurmountable.

And it will be deemed unwise to share a lover's performance problems outside of one's circle of true girlfriends. For disloyal and wanton women might receive that information as a challenge and try to "cure" him at the next party.

Lo, and let us be reminded that sometimes, by unfortunate happenstance, sexual rapture will elude us, even if a man is divinely endowed and seemingly adept in the ways of the flesh. And this, too, we hope and pray, shall pass.

For, woe, if this does not pass and you resolve to spare yourself this man's rod and spoil the affair, I will offer you my steadfast support. For we are put on this earth too short a time to waste it on a man who cannot deliver us to the Promised Land. And to that I say, "Amen, sister!"

The Book of Mary

And the angel appeared to Mary,

who had just returned from a date with yet another loser sheepherder. Mary was filled with angst and sadness because shepherds were notoriously cheap, fearful of commitment, and hygiene-challenged, and she was weary of always smelling like wet wool and mutton. "Behold the good news, Mary!" the angel said, "For I have found you the perfect man. A man who will love you so much, he will sacrifice his ass for you, in the most literal sense! See?" And Mary, after examining Joseph's dowry, which happened to be grazing in her front yard, asked, "What does this man look like?" and was assured by the angel that Joseph was handsome, good, and, most importantly, had nothing to do with sheep, professionally speaking. And thus Mary and Joseph met, fell in love, and rode off into the sunset to start a family. And the rest is history.

And if it comes to pass that one of us finds a man whom we adore and who is willing to commit to us for eternity, it shall be cause for rejoicing throughout the land.

And if you are fortunate enough to take such a man, I will welcome him with open arms. And I will not reveal the sordid stories of your past, no matter how luscious, to your new love or his family. Because you possess as much dirt on me as I possess on you. And I am no fool.

And if you decide to enter into matrimony with this man, I will celebrate with unbridled enthusiasm. And I will joyfully wear the bridesmaid frock of your choosing. And it will matter not if the frock is repulsive and I will never have occasion to wear it again. My lips shall be sealed.

And I will stand up for you at the ceremonial altar and hold your bouquet and whisper in your ear when it is time to say "I do." And I will assure you that it is nerves that are causing your tears, not bridal remorse. And it will all be good.

And when the time comes, I will raise my glass high and toast you, your beloved, and your future together. And I will be careful not to mention, no matter how loose-lipped I am from the champagne, how many frogs you had to kiss before you found your prince or what really came to pass on our bachelorette weekend in Vegas.

For I know that your future will, indeed, still include me. Perhaps not with the same frequency of club-hopping and vodka tonics, but with a friendship that will withstand the test of time, testosterone, and toddlers.

For in the beginning,

there were girlfriends. And girlfriends there will be, forever and ever. Amen.

Love ya!
Karen